Whose Equipment Is This?

by Amanda Doering Tourville

Consulting editor: Gail Saunders-Smith, PhD

CAPSTONE PRESS
a capstone imprint

Pebble Plus is published by Capstone Press,
151 Good Counsel Drive, P.O. Box 669, Mankato, Minnesota 56002.
www.capstonepub.com

Books published by Capstone Press are manufactured with paper
containing at least 10 percent post-consumer waste.

Library of Congress Cataloging-in-Publication Data
Tourville, Amanda Doering, 1980–
  Whose equipment is this? / by Amanda Doering Tourville.
      p. cm.—(Pebble plus books. Community helper mysteries)
  Includes bibliographical references and index.
  Summary: "Simple text and full-color photographs present a mystery community helper, one clue at a time, until his or
her identity is revealed"—Provided by publisher.
  ISBN 978-1-4296-6080-8 (library binding)
  1. Police—Juvenile literature. I. Title. II. Series.
  HV7922.T683 2012
  363.2—dc22   2011005504

Editorial Credits
Jeni Wittrock, editor; Matt Bruning and Bobbie Nuytten, designers; Wanda Winch, media researcher;
    Laura Manthe, production specialist; Sarah Schuette, photo stylist; Marcy Morin, photo scheduler

Photo Credits
All photos by Capstone Studio/Karon Dubke except:
Shutterstock: mypokcik, puzzle design element, Scott Rothstein, cover, 1

Capstone would like to thank the North Mankato Police Department for their assistance with the photos in this book.

Note to Parents and Teachers

The Community Helper Mysteries set supports social studies standards related to communities.
This book describes and illustrates police officers. The images support early readers in
understanding the text. The repetition of words and phrases helps early readers learn new
words. This book also introduces early readers to subject-specific vocabulary words, which are
defined in the Glossary section. Early readers may need assistance to read some words and to
use the Table of Contents, Glossary, Read More, Internet Sites, and Index sections of the book.

Printed in the United States of America in North Mankato, Minnesota.
032011   006110CGF11

Table of Contents

It's a Mystery

This book is full of clues
about me. I'm a helper
in your community.
Can you guess what I do?

Here's your first clue:
Sometimes I work inside
a building. Other times
I work outdoors.

When I'm working outdoors,

I need transportation.

I may walk, drive a car,

or ride a motorcycle.

I may even ride a horse.

I can work alone or with
a partner. Usually my co-worker
is another person. But sometimes
my partner is a dog!

What I Wear

My uniform is a shirt, pants, and a belt. Sometimes I wear a hat. I wear shoes that help me run fast if I need to.

Equipment I Use

I carry equipment to keep people safe. I use the equipment to stop anyone who tries to harm others.

How I Can Help

If you are lost, look for me.

I'll help you find your family

and get home safely.

15

If there is an emergency,

I will race to get there.

I take charge and make sure

everyone gets the help they need.

I make sure the streets are safe.

People who drive too fast may

get a ticket.

Have you guessed who I am?

Mystery Solved!

I'm a police officer!

This community helper mystery is solved!

Glossary

emergency—a sudden and dangerous situation that must be handled quickly

equipment—the machines and tools needed for a job or an activity

ticket—a written order to pay a fine for breaking a traffic law

transportation—a way to move from one place to another

uniform—special clothes that members of a particular group wear

Read More

Ames, Michelle. *Police Officers in Our Community.* On the Job. New York: PowerKids Press, 2010.

Armentrout, David, and Patricia Armentrout. *The Police Station.* Our Community. Vero Beach, Fla.: Rourke Pub., 2009.

Rau, Dana Meachen. *Police Officer.* Benchmark Rebus. New York: Marshall Cavendish Benchmark, 2008.

Internet Sites

FactHound offers a safe, fun way to find Internet sites related to this book. All of the sites on FactHound have been researched by our staff.

Here's all you do:

Visit *www.facthound.com*

Type in this code: 9781429660808

Check out projects, games and lots more at
www.capstonekids.com

Index

Word Count: 196
Grade: 1
Early-Intervention Level: 17